WILLIAM BYRD

MASS

for 4 Voices
für 4 Stimmen
Edited by/Herausgegeben von
Frederick Hudson

T0081221

Ernst Eulenburg Ltd
London · Mainz · New York · Paris · Tokyo · Zürich

Contents

Preface   I

Editorial notes   VI

Vorwort VIII

Facsimile of 1st edition of 1592-3   IX

Facsimile of 2nd edition of c.1599   X

Dedication   XI

Kyrie eleison   I

Gloria in excelsis..   5

Credo   21

Sanctus   44

Benedictus   49

Agnus Dei   53

William Byrd: Latin Masses for Four, Three and Five Voices

The present critical editions of Byrd's three Latin Masses are the result of a search made over the past few years in an attempt to locate all extant printed sources of his lifetime and contemporary and later copies in manuscript, and to collate these with all editions which have appeared since. The editor is greatly indebted to the late William A. Jackson, Harvard University Library, and to his staff who are currently revising the *Short-Title Catalogue . . . 1475–1640*, and who made available pre-publication information concerning the present location of all copies of Byrd's published works. Printed sources of the Masses are held by the British Museum, Christ Church (Oxford), Bodleian Library, Cambridge University Library, Lincoln Cathedral Library, Folger Shakespeare Library (Washington, D.C.), the Library of Congress, and by these only. The editor has visited the editorial headquarters of the *Répertoire International des Sources Musicales* for the West (Kassel), and for the East (Berlin), to check whether printed sources are extant elsewhere, but results have proved negative. As the provenance of the American holdings was England until recently, and as all other copies are held in this country, their absence in continental libraries would seem to argue that Byrd did not seek a market abroad for his Masses as H. Washington and other editors have suggested. The English sources have been inspected in person, including typographical comparisons and recording of the paper and watermarks, and the editor wishes to express warm appreciation to Miss Dorothy Mason and Dr. W. Lichtenwanger (Folger, and Library of Congress respectively) for generous provision of detailed information during a long correspondence. The editor has gathered photocopies of all printed sources of the Masses (a total of 61 part-books) and of the MS copies in the Fitzwilliam Museum and British Museum, together with copies of all later editions (photographic where these are out of print). The sources and later editions are listed and described below under the respective Masses.

At the beginning of this search the editor was fortunate in learning from Dr. H. K. Andrews† that he had recently made the significant discovery of the existence of two distinct editions of the *Mass for Four Voices* and the *Mass for Three Voices* respectively. Up to the present, editors of these Masses have assumed that Byrd published them in one edition only of each Mass and, from comments in their prefaces and comparisons of their music texts, it can be proved that their editions have been founded on copies of the 2nd edition. Further, it can be proved that editors, (with the possible exception of Leo Manzetti, Ohio), have consulted solely the British Museum holdings *K.8.d.11* (4-part, 2nd edition) and *K.8.d.10* (3-part, 2nd edition), even though the Royal Music Library copies of the 1st edition have been available in the BM for consultation since 1911, and other copies of the 1st edition of the 4-part Mass are located in Christ Church, Lincoln Cathedral and the Folger libraries. On the other hand, a collation of the printed sources of the *Mass for Five Voices* shows that the copies are identical in every respect, including the paper and watermarks, and there is no evidence to indicate that this Mass appeared in a second edition.

The 61 part-books of the five editions of the three Masses all lack titlepages and it may be assumed that they were issued without them: it is sufficiently remarkable that Latin Masses were printed at all in England at this period. The facsimile reproductions show that the number of voices, the voice part, and Byrd's name are printed at the top of each page. No publisher is named but a comparison of the type and ornamental capitals points without doubt to Thomas East, who was the sole publisher of Byrd's works between 1588 and 1607 known to us. The most obvious difference between the 1st and 2nd editions of the 4-part and 3-part Masses respectively is that the 1st editions bear the barred ₵ time signature while the 2nd editions have the unbarred C signature. Dr. Andrews has shown in his article, *Printed Sources of Byrd's "Psalmes, Sonets and Songs"*, (M & L 44, Jan. 1963, pp. 5–20), that both of these signatures represent $\frac{4}{2}$, that when they were used in all voices throughout a work they had no proportional significance and were interchangeable, and that the change from the barred to the unbarred signature for works in imperfect time occurred in English publications from about 1594–5 onwards. The next point of comparison is that the same ornamental capital initials (in *K*yrie, *E*t in terra, *P*atrem, *S*anctus, and *A*gnus) were used in all voice parts of all five editions, that is, that East possessed only one block for each ornamental capital. This postulates that East dispersed the type of one part-book before the next could be set up and printed: this is proved by a comparison of the equivalent voice parts of the 1st and 2nd editions of the 4-part and 3-part Masses—the type of the 2nd editions has been completely reset in every page of these two issues. It must be emphasized here that the notation of the respective 1st editions is remarkably accurate, (like the 1st edition of *Psalmes, Sonets and Songs*, 1588), and that the few misprints which have crept into the 2nd editions are probably due to lack of care in composing the type from 1st edition "copy", and lack of the careful proof-reading received by the 1st editions. (In the *Sanctus*, 4-part Mass, Altus, bar 3, H. Washington is the only editor to correct the 2nd edition misprint as it appears in the 1st edition: Rockstro and Squire leave the error unchanged, and Fellowes and TCM vol. 9 give an impossible solution.)

The dating of the three Masses has hitherto been conjectural in all editions. Thanks are due to Mr. P. J. Clulow, who has worked in collaboration with the late Dr. Andrews, for a comprehensive survey of Thomas East's publications based on a detailed comparison of typographical features, and which has finally produced convincing dates. His methods, results and conclusions are published in the recent article, *Publication Dates for Byrd's Latin Masses*, (M & L 47, Jan. 1966, pp 1–9), which should be consulted for full information. Important evidence includes the change from the barred to the unbarred time signature about 1594–5, defined by the late Dr. Andrews' article, and the gradual wear on the face of the ornamental capitals. Mr. Clulow's chronology may be summarized as follows:

Mass	Edition	Time Signature	Published
4 voices	1st	₵	early in the period 1592–3;
3 voices	1st	₵	late in the period 1593–4;
5 voices	sole	₵	probably about 1595;
4 voices	2nd	C	⎱ about 5 years later than the 1st
3 voices	2nd	C	⎰ editions, probably c. 1599.

THE PRESENT EDITIONS

NOTE VALUES: The original time signatures, ₵ and C, both imply a modern equivalent of $\frac{4}{2}$, *i.e.* a minim "tactus" or pulse. In accordance with modern custom the note values have been halved, giving a time signature of $\frac{4}{4}$ with a crotchet tactus.

BARRING: As there are overwhelming historical and practical reasons for regular barring, these editions have adopted a system of regular units of four pulses. Even though no bar-lines were used in the original part-books, (except at the end of sections and movements), the rests which occur before and during the course of the voice parts are, without exception, carefully ordered so that units of two minim pulses occur from beginning to end, (*e.g.* two separate minim rests are placed between phrases where one semibreve rest might have been indicated—a weak tactus followed by a strong one with an implied "bar-line" between the two rests). Further, where there is a long series of rests printed at the beginning or during the course of a voice part, an additional warning sign in the form of a colon appears before the last strong minim rest—again an implied "bar-line". Finally the organ-books of 16th century motets, anthems, &c, at Durham, Ely, Peterhouse, Tenbury and Christ Church, though barred irregularly, invariably contain an even number of minims within the bar-lines. On practical grounds, changes of time signature and uneven bar lengths are not immediately obvious to or easily handled by singers, choirs and choir directors. Fellowes' post-1923 editions show a change of outlook from his earlier practice of irregular bar lengths. Experience has proved to the present editor that cross rhythms and agogic accents are easier to feel and interpret when the barring is regular—the choristers sing against the regular bar-lines with a sense of lilt!

DYNAMICS, PACE AND EXPRESSION INDICATIONS: No performing indications have been added in order that choir directors and singers may have clean scores to interpret as they wish. Occasionally, where the accent is not immediately obvious in a cross rhythm, the editor has placed a short line (–) above or below the appropriate note.

VERBAL TEXT AND UNDERLAYING: Where the words in the printed sources appear in full they are reproduced in the present editions in direct print. Where the sign, *ij*, is used in these sources to indicate a repetition of a phrase, the words are reproduced in cursive (italic) print. A comparison of the two editions of the 4-part and 3-part Masses, however, has rarely left the editor in doubt concerning the underlaying, either in the full texts or the repeats. Though the printed sources use small initial letters for certain words referring to the Deity, (*Deus pater, agnus Dei, spiritus sancto,* &c, &c), where one would expect capitals, the 19 different part-books of the five Mass editions are wholly consistent in printing capitals for the words *Catholicam et Apostolicam Ecclesiam* in the Creed, as though this were a special affirmation of faith in the usurped Church, and suggests that Byrd gave instructions to this end or paid special attention to this in his proof-reading.

ACCIDENTALS: A study of the printed sources, especially of the 1st editions of the 4-part and 3-part Masses, has convinced the editor that Byrd meant what he printed, and that there is very little to be added in the way of accidentals. Accidentals which are placed before the notes in the present edition appear in the printed sources. Two forms of editorial accidentals have been used, (a) placed above the notes where there may be the slightest doubt and where the sharpening of the note below the leading note has been forgotten or presumed, and (b) placed in brackets before the note where the inference is quite clear, *e.g.* on the reversion to the note proper to the mode after a tierce de picardie cadence, or as a warning sign to singers in performance.

LIGATURES: Though the use and effect of ligatures were somewhat archaic if not obsolete by this period, the places where they occur have been indicated by square brackets placed above the appropriate notes.

INTONATIONS: As aids to performance the editor has suggested traditional plainsong intonations to the *Gloria in excelsis* and *Credo* which are suitable for the Aeolian mode (4-part and 5-part Masses) and the Ionian mode (3-part Mass). Others may be found in the *Liber Usualis*, edited by the Benedictines of Solesmes, Paris, &c, 1956 pp. 16ff and 64ff.

TRANSPOSITION AND VOICE RANGES: The compass of the voice parts is extraordinarily wide in each of the Masses, and would appear to embrace both Morley's "high key" and "low key" at one and the same time, (*Plaine and Easie Introduction to Practicall Musick*, 1597, p. 166; reprint edited by R. A. Harman, 1952, p. 274f). The 4-part Mass has been transposed down a whole tone, but the 3-part and 5-part Masses have been printed in their original untransposed modes. An interesting and plausible theory of *chiavette* transposition is put forward by the late H. K. Andrews in *Transposition of Byrd's Vocal Polyphony*, (M & L 43, 1962, pp. 25–37). Though there are historical and aesthetic reasons why a true modern transposition should be observed, nevertheless choir directors (especially of choirs with female altos) will perform these works in whatever transposition suits the greatest number of voices.

CHAMBER ORGAN CONTINUO AND REHEARSAL ACCOMPANIMENT: In each of the Masses the editor has provided a simplified *reductio partiturae* for the use of choirs which need some keyboard assistance at rehearsals. At the same time there is historical evidence that Byrd used, or intended to be used, some form of keyboard continuo in the performance of these Masses. This evidence is based on performing procedure in church music of this period, and consideration of the purpose for which Byrd composed music for the proscribed "papistical rites" in the light of a review of his published Latin works, their pitch and vocal compasses. The organ-books at Christ Church, Durham, Peterhouse and elsewhere, and the fact that the Chapel Royal, Durham, York, and other cathedrals and collegiate churches maintained consorts of cornetts and sackbuts to double the voices, provide sufficient proof that it was not customary to perform church music unaccompanied. In the Reformed Churches in England the performance of Latin works was by no means forbidden where the language was understood, but the *Booke of Common Praier* was to be adhered to for liturgical services, and such Latin works as were uncontroversial had an extra-liturgical place. In this category one may place the *Cantiones Sacrae*, 1575, dedicated to Queen Elizabeth, to which Tallis and Byrd each contributed 17 motets, and the two books of *Sacrarum Cantionum*, 1589 and 1591, which contain 16 and 21 motets respectively. An analysis of these 54 Byrd motets shows that, with the possible exception of *Salve, Regina, Mater*, (1591, No. 6), the texts are uncontroversial, and the pitches and vocal compasses lie in such a low range that Byrd must have written them in organ (or church) pitch with performance in the Reformed Church as a possibility, if not a fact, and postulating a modern transposition of a whole tone or a minor third higher. On the other hand, the two books of *Gradualia*, 1605 and 1607, with a 2nd edition of each appearing in 1610, between them contain the Proper of the Mass (Introit, Gradual, Alleluia or Tract, Offertory, and Communion) together with certain Responsories at Vespers, for the Festivals of one whole year, including the Festivals of the BVM and other festivals not included in the reformed Prayer Book. In the preface to the first book of *Gradualia* Byrd states that these are . . . "for you who delight at times to sing to God in hymns and spiritual songs . . .", and it may be argued that his purpose was nostalgic and not practical. It is far more likely, however, that these 107 Introits, &c, were in fact performed, at least in part, at secret celebrations of the old rites in manor houses and other private dwellings, and the same may be claimed for his settings of the Mass for 4, 3 and 5 voices. That the 4-part and 3-part Masses went into a 2nd edition, like the *Gradualia* some ten years later, could be put forward as supporting evidence of demand for and use in such celebrations, and cannot be wholly explained away as nostalgic. An analysis of the pitches and vocal compasses of the Masses and *Gradualia* shows them to be in the same category, namely that they lie within the vocal compasses of the church choir (with male altos) without the usual transposition of a whole tone or a minor third higher for modern performance, and were therefore not written at organ pitch (*i.e.* the pitch of the organs in the Reformed Churches). The corollary is that the Masses and *Gradualia* were written at secular pitch and, if they were performed at all (which the editor considers highly probable), that they were accompanied by a chamber organ according to the normal procedure for performing church music, or, failing this, that use was made of a consort of viols. (This analysis of pitches and compasses has taken into consideration the possibility that Byrd made a distinction in certain items of the *Gradualia* between "high key"—*"for more life"*, and "low key"—*"for more gravity and staidness"*, as set out in the contemporary publication of his pupil Morley, and that in a few items he has observed the modal limitations of the respective voices—an archaic practice by this time.) Modern performances of the Masses and *Gradualia*, on the contrary, frequently demand a transposition to a lower key as, for example, in the present edition of the 4-part Mass.

Choir directors will naturally perform the three Masses with or without chamber organ continuo as they see fit, but it is hoped that a case has been stated for the historical truth of the organ continuo as something more than speculation. It is not generally realized that the English tradition of singing 16th century works un- accompanied is not much older than the English Renaissance of the end of the last century, when editors began to make such comments as . . . *Accompt. for practice only* (Rockstro & Squire, 4-pt Mass, 1890), and . . . *should always be sung without accompaniment* (Squire, 3-pt Mass, 1901). The authentic tradition of accompanied singing survived through the 17th century to the 19th: John Immyns' MS score of the 3-part Mass which he made for his Madrigal Society c. 1750 has a figured bass (Fitzwilliam Museum MS *30.G.5*), and the first edition of a Byrd Mass since the 16th century (Rimbault, 5-part, 1841) has a companion organ-part made by Mac- farren. The organ-score at Christ Church (*Ch.Ch.1001*), written early in the 17th century and containing nothing later than the works of Gibbons, is not merely a transcription of the voice parts but introduces decorations and passing notes freely. When it is decided to use an organ in modern performance, the continuo player should therefore use his discretion in decorating the chamber organ part provided by the present editor, for example, playing decorated resolutions of suspended dis- cords instead of plain, and the reverse. In any case, the continuo should be light, it should blend with the voices unobtrusively, and pedals should not be used.

Serious students of Byrd's style are commended to H. K. Andrews' monumental, posthumous publication, *The Technique of Byrd's Vocal Polyphony*, pp. 306, 4°, OUP 1966, (568 music examples): Byrd's use of the "head-motif" in his Masses is discussed on p. 267ff.

MASS FOR FOUR VOICES

SOURCES

A: 1st edition of 1592–3, Thomas East; *CANTUS, ALTUS, TENOR, BASSUS,* each of 4 folios, size 21½ × 15½ cms; time signature: ₵. Three complete and two incomplete sets of part-books are extant:—

- *(a)* Christ Church, Oxford: *Ch.Ch.491, 489, 492, 493.* Each part bears the inscription: *Homo cum sis, id fac semper intelligas. Thomas Holbech.* There was a Thomas Holbech at Trinity College, 1681–4, and it is probable that Henry Aldrich, Dean of Christ Church, 1689–1710, acquired this set from him and had it bound up with other Byrd works in these part-books.
- *(b)* Folger Shakespeare Library, Washington, D.C: *STC 4250.* The provenance of this set is first, Britwell Court, and then the Harmsworth Collection, purchased by the Folger Library in 1937.
- *(c)* Lincoln Cathedral Library: *Mm.4/5, 4/7, 4/8, 4/9.* The editor has the impression that the prints in these part-books were bound together during the first half of the 17th century.
- *(d)* British Museum, Royal Music Library (on permanent loan since 1911, presented outright in 1957): *R.M.15.d.5* (lacks Altus).
- *(e)* Library of Congress, Washington, D.C: *M 1490. S 69 Case* (Bassus only). Bound in a miscellaneous collection of bass parts under the binder's title, "Songs, Madrigals, Ballads, etc.".

B: 2nd edition of c. 1599, Thomas East, type completely reset; part-books, folios and size of folios as in 1st edition; time signature: *C.* One complete and two incomplete sets are extant:—

- *(a)* British Museum: *K.8.d.11.* Acquired 1888.
- *(b)* Bodleian Library, Oxford: *Douce MM 361 (15)* (Tenor only).
- *(c)* Cambridge University Library: *Syn.6.58.13* (Cantus only).

EDITIONS

C: 1890: W. S. Rockstro & W. B. Squire, *Mass in F minor,* Novello. Transposed down one tone, original note values (minim tactus), bar units of two minims. Founded on source *B(a).*

D: 1922: E. H. Fellowes, *Mass for Four Voices,* Stainer & Bell. Transposed down one tone, original note values (minim tactus), bar units of 4, 6 and 8 minims. Founded on source *B(a).* The plates of this edition were used without change for the reprint in *Collected Works of Byrd,* Vol. I, pp. 30–67, Stainer & Bell, 1937.

E.1: 1923: E. H. Fellowes, *The Office for the Holy Communion adapted to English Words from the Msss for Four Voices,* Stainer & Bell. Transposed down one tone, original note values (minim tactus), bar units as in *D.* No new sources used.

E.2: 1938: E. H. Fellowes, *The Office for the Holy Communion . . .* as in *E.1,* Stainer & Bell. Transposed down one tone, note values halved (crochet tactus), bar units now mainly of 4 crotchets but with occasional bars of 6 and 8 crotchets, otherwise as *E.1.*

F: 1928: Buck, Fellowes, Ramsbotham & Warner, *Tudor Church Music,* Vol. 9, p. 17, Carnegie Trust & OUP. Original pitch and note values (minim tactus), bar units of 4, 6 and 8 minims. Founded on source *B(a).*

G; 1959: H. Washington, *Mass for Four Voices,* J. & W. Chester. Transposed down one tone, note values halved (crotchet tactus), bar units of four crotchets with occasional bars of 2 crotchets. Founded on source *B(a).*

TEXTUAL CRITICISM

The following comments refer chiefly to the printed sources *A* and *B,* with references to important differences in editions *C* to *G.*

Bar	Voice	"KYRIE ELEISON"
7	Altus	A, B: No accidental before last note and accepted as correct; note sharpened in *C* to *G* inclusive.
7–8	Altus	A: *eleyson;* B: *eleison*
7–10	Tenor	A, B: *eleyson*
8–10	Bassus	A, B: *eleyson*

		"GLORIA IN EXCELSIS"
50	Bassus	B: 2nd note misprinted 3rd lower; corrected in *C* to *G*
110	Tenor	A: *solus;* B: *solous*
125	Tenor	C: 1st and 2nd notes: *g* (one beat) substituted because of "false relation" of *e* and *e flat*
		F: 2nd note sharpened (leap of diminished 4th)

Bar	Voice	**"CREDO"**
40	Altus	G: last note: editorial natural added
45–6	Altus	A: *ommia*; B: *omnia*
52	Bassus	B: note misprinted 3rd lower; corrected in *C* to *G*
59–62	Cantus	A, B: *caelis*
60–62	Bassus	A, B: *celis*
61–62	Tenor	A, B: *celis*
63	Altus	A: *in Carnatus*; B: *in carnatus*
64	Tenor	A, B: *in Carnatus*
67	Cantus	A: *Spiritu*; B: *spiritu*
75–76	Altus Tenor	} C: these voices rewritten, partly through interchange
76	Cantus	C, G: 2nd note: editorial natural added
88	Tenor	D, E.1, E.2: 2nd and 3rd notes changed to *f'* and *g'*
100	Cantus	A: *sedit*; B: *sedet*
150	Tenor	A: *unam*; B: *unum*
173ff	All voices	A, B: *seculi*

"SANCTUS"

3	Altus	A: 2nd note as in present edition (perfect 5th below 1st note); B: misprinted semitone higher; C: follows B; D, E.1, E.2, F: *f'* substituted; G: sole correct emendation
15ff	Bassus	A, B: *sabaoth*

"BENEDICTUS"

51–52	Tenor	A: *venet*; B: *venit*
58	Altus	A: *domini*; B: *Domini*

"AGNUS DEI"

31–32	Bassus	A, B: *dei*

In both *A* and *B* the final note of sections and movements in all voice parts is printed as a "long", irrespective of whether all voices arrive at the final note at the same time, and thus having the effect of a pause. Choir directors should therefore feel at liberty to hold final chords at discretion.

For willing collaboration and facilities afforded, warmest thanks are expressed to the following, in addition to those already named: Mr. A. H. King, Mr. O. W. Neighbour, (British Museum); Miss P. J. Willetts (BM Dept of MSS); Dr. D. M. Rogers (Bodleian Library); Mr. H. J. R. Wing (Christ Church Library); Mr. H. R. Creswick (Cambridge University Library); Miss P. M. Giles (Fitzwilliam Museum); Mr. C. Cudworth (Music School, Cambridge); Canon H. F. Riches, Dr. G. A. Slater (Lincoln Cathedral); Dr. F. W. Riedel (Kassel); Dr. K. H. Köhler (Berlin); Cheflektor H. Schulze (B & H, Leipzig); Mr. A. D. Bonner (Stainer & Bell, London); Mr. B. Dunne (Burns & Oates, London); Miss K. F. Pantzer (Harvard University Library); Revd. Dr. E. Harriott (Newcastle); Revd. Fr. B. Harriott (South Shields); Dr. W. S. Mitchell (Newcastle University Library).

The University,
Newcastle upon Tyne,   FREDERICK HUDSON
February 1966.

Vorwort
William Byrd: Drei lateinische Messen

(vierstimmig, dreistimmig und fünfstimmig)

Die vorliegende kritische Ausgabe der drei lateinischen Messen von Byrd ist das Forschungsergebnis der letzten Jahre, ausgehend von dem Versuch, alle vorhandenen gedruckten Quellen aus Byrds Lebenszeit und alle zeitgenössischen und späteren handschriftlichen Kopien aufzufinden und sie mit den seither erschienenen Ausgaben zu vergleichen. Der Herausgeber ist William A. Jackson†, Harvard University Library, zu grossem Dank verpflichtet, ebenso dessen Mitarbeitern, die laufend den *Short-Title Catalogue . . . 1475–1640* revidieren, für die vor der Veröffentlichung erteilte Auskunft über die heutige Lokalisierung aller publizierten Werke von Byrd. Gedruckte Vorlagen der Messen befinden sich ausschliesslich in folgenden Bibliotheken: British Museum, Christ Church (Oxford), Bodleian Library, Cambridge University Library, Lincoln Cathedral Library, Folger Shakespeare Library (Washington, D.C.), Library of Congress. Der Herausgeber hat die Schriftleitungen der *Répertoire International des Sources Musicales* in Kassel (für den Westen) und in Berlin (für den Osten) aufgesucht, um festzustellen, ob noch weitere gedruckte Quellen anderswo existieren, aber mit negativem Erfolg. Aus der Tatsache, dass alle amerikanischen Exemplare sich bis vor kurzem in England befanden und dass die übrigen in England sind und in den kontinentalen Bibliotheken fehlen, scheint zu folgen, dass Byrd keinen Absatz für seine Messen im Ausland suchte, wie H. Washington und andere Herausgeber vermutet haben. Der Herausgeber hat persönlich die englischen Quellen eingesehen, typographisch verglichen und Papier und Wasserzeichen registriert und möchte hiermit Miss Dorothy Mason und Dr. W. Lichtenwanger (Folger, und Library of Congress) herzlich danken für viele eingehende Informationen während der langen Korrespondenz. Er hat fernerhin Fotokopien aller gedruckten Quellen der Messen (alles in allem 61 Stimmbücher) gesammelt und ebenfalls die handschriftlichen Kopien im Fitzwilliam Museum und British Museum, und Exemplare aller späteren Ausgaben (Photographien, wenn vergriffen). Die Quellen und späteren Ausgaben sind unten bei den einzelnen Messen aufgezählt und beschrieben.

Am Anfang seiner Forschung wurde der Herausgeber von Herrn Dr. H. K. Andrews† freundlicherweise daraufhingewiesen, dass dieser vor kurzem die wichtige Entdeckung von der Existenz je zweier verschiedener Ausgaben der 4 stimmigen und der 3 stimmigen Messen gemacht hatte. Bisher hatten die Herausgeber dieser Messen angenommen, dass Byrd sie nur in je einer Ausgabe veröffentlicht hatte. Aus Bemerkungen in ihren Einleitungen und Vergleichen der Texte lässt sich beweisen, dass ihre Ausgaben sich auf Kopien der 2. Ausgabe gründen. Ferner lässt sich beweisen, dass alle Herausgeber (wohl mit Ausnahme von Leo Manzetti, Ohio) nur die Quellen des British Museum *K.8.d.11* (4 stimmig, 2. Auflage) und *K.8.d.10.* (3 stimmig, 2. Auflage) benutzt haben, obwohl die Kopien der 1. Ausgabe in der Royal Music Library im British Museum seit 1911 zur Verfügung standen und ebenso andere Kopien der 1. Ausgabe der 4 stimmigen Messe in den Bibliotheken der Christ Church College, der Cathedrale in Lincoln und der Folger Bibliothek. Andererseits zeigt ein Vergleich der gedruckten Quellen der 5 stimmigen Messe, dass die Kopien in jeder Hinsicht identisch sind, einschliesslich Papier und Wasserzeichen; nichts deutet daraufhin, dass diese Messe in einer 2. Ausgabe erschien.

In allen 61 Stimmbüchern der 5 Ausgaben dieser drei Messen fehlen die Titelseiten; offenbar sind sie ohne die herausgegeben worden. Dass lateinische Messen überhaupt in dieser Zeit in England gedruckt wurden, ist ungewöhnlich genug. Die Faksimiles zeigen, dass die Anzahl der Stimmen, die Stimme selbst und Byrds Name oben auf jeder Seite gedruckt sind. Ein Verleger ist nicht genannt, aber der Vergleich der Typen und der verzierten Anfangsbuchstaben deutet zweifellos auf Thomas East hin, den einzigen uns bekannten Verleger von Byrds Werken zwischen 1588 und 1607. Der auffallendste Unterschied zwischen den 1. und 2. Ausgaben der 4 stimmigen und der 3 stimmigen Messe ist der, dass die 1. Ausgaben das durchstrichene C als Zeitmass (C), die zweiten es undurchstrichen haben. In seinem Aufsatz *Printed Sources of Byrd's "Psalmes, Sonets and Songs"*, (M & L 44, Jan. 1963, pp 5–20) hat Dr. Andrews nachgeweisen, dass diese beiden Zeitmasse $\frac{4}{2}$ bedeuten und dass, wenn sie durch ein ganzes Werk hindurch in allen Stimmen stehen, sie keinerlei proportionale Bedeutung haben und austauschbar sind, und dass der Wechsel vom durchstrichenen zum undurchstrichenen C in Werken im tempus imperfectum etwa 1594–95 zum ersten Mal in englischen Drucken vorkommt. Der nächste Vergleichspunkt ist der, dass die gleichen verzierten Anfangsbuchstaben (in *Kyrie*, *Et* in terra, *Patrem*, *Sanctus* und *Agnus*) in allen Stimmen aller fünf Ausgaben benutzt wurden, was bedeutet, dass East nur eine Type für jeden verzierten Anfangsbuchstaben hatte. Daraus kann man folgern, dass East die Type eines Stimmbuches absetzte, bevor das nächste gesetzt und gedruckt werden

konnte; das wird bewiesen durch einen Vergleich der entsprechenden Stimmen der 1. und 2. Ausgaben der 3 und 4 stimmigen Messen: die zweiten Ausgaben sind auf jeder Seite beider Messen völlig neu gesetzt. Hier muss betont werden, dass die Notierung der jeweiligen ersten Ausgaben erstaunlich genau ist (wie die erste Ausgabe der *Psalmes, Sonets and Songs*, 1588), und dass die wenigen Druckfehler, die sich in die zweiten Ausgaben einschlichen, wahrscheinlich durch nachlässiges Setzen nach einem Exemplar der ersten Ausgabe entstanden sind und durch das Fehlen des sorfältigen Korrekturlesens, das die ersten Ausgaben erfahren hatten. (Im *Sanctus*, 4 stimmige Messe, Altus, Takt 3 ist H. Washington der einzige Herausgeber, der den Druckfehler der zweiten Ausgabe korrigiert, der ersten Ausgabe entsprechend. Rockstro und Squire lassen den Fehler stehen und Fellowes und TCM vol. 9 geben eine unmögliche Lösung.)

Die Datierung der drei Messen beruhte bisher in allen Ausgaben auf Mutmassung. Dank gebührt Mr. P. J. Clulow, dem Mitarbeiter des verstorbenen Dr. Andrews, für seinen umfassenden Überblick über Thomas Easts Publikationen, die auf einem eingehenden Vergleich von typographischen Merkmalen basiert und endlich überzeugende Daten bringt. Seine Methoden, Resultate und Schlussfolgerungen sind kürzlich veröffentlicht worden in dem Artikel *Publication Dates for Byrd's Latin Masses* (M & L 47, Jan. 1966, pp 1–9) und sollten zur genauen Information herangezogen werden. Das wichtige Beweismaterial schliesst den Wechsel vom durchstrichenen zum undurchstrichenen Zeitmass um 1594–95 ein, wie es in Dr. Andrews Artikel beschrieben ist, und die allmähliche Abnutzung der Oberfläche der verzierten Anfangsbuchstaben. Mr. Clulows chronologische Reihenfolge kann wie folgt zusammengefasst werden:

X

Messe	Ausgabe	Zeitmass	Publiziert
4 Stimmen	1.	₵	1592–3;
3 Stimmen	1.	₵	1593–4;
5 Stimmen	Einzige	₵	ca. 1595;
4 Stimmen	2.	C	ca. 5 Jahre
3 Stimmen	2.	C	später als die
			1. Ausgabe, um 1599.

DIE VORLIEGENDEN AUSGABEN

NOTENWERTE: Die ursprünglichen Taktvorzeichen ₵ und C gleichen dem heutigen $\frac{4}{2}$ d.h. dem "tactus" oder Taktschlag einer Halben. In Übereinstimmung mit dem heutigen Brauch sind die Notenwerte halbiert worden und geben ein Taktvorzeichen von $\frac{4}{4}$ mit einem Tactus von einem Viertel.

TAKTEINTEILUNG: Da überzeugende historische und praktische Gründe für regelmässige Takte vorhanden sind, ist in diesen Ausgaben ein System der regelmässigen Einheiten von vier Taktschlägen angewendet worden. Obwohl die originalen Stimmbücher keine Taktstriche haben (ausgenommen am Ende von Abschnitten und Sätzen), sind die Pausen in und vor den Stimmen ausnahmslos so sorgfältig angeordnet, dass Einheiten von zwei halben Taktschlägen sich vom Anfang bis zum Ende ergeben, (z.B. zwei gesonderte halbe Pausen sind zwischen Phrasen gesetzt, wo eine ganze Pause angebracht wäre—ein schwacher Tactus gefolgt von einem starken, mit einem imaginären Taktstrich zwischen den beiden Pausen). Fernerhin, wo eine lange Serie von Pausen vor oder innerhalb einer Stimme gedruckt ist, erscheint ein zusätzliches Warnungszeichen in der Form eines Doppelpunktes vor der letzten halben Pause— wiederum ein imaginärer Taktstrich. Zum Schluss: die Orgelbücher der Motetten und Anthems etc. des 16. Jahrhunderts in Durham, Peterhouse, Ely, Tenbury und Christ Church, obwohl mit unregelmässig eingeteilten Takten, enthalten durchgehend eine gerade Anzahl von Halben innerhalb der Taktstriche. In der Praxis sind Wechsel von Taktvorzeichen und ungleiche Taktlängen für den Sänger, für Chöre und Chordirigenten nicht leicht zu erkennen und zu bewältigen. Fellowes Ausgaben nach 1923 zeigen eine Meinungsänderung von seiner früheren Praxis unregelmässig langer Takte. Erfahrung hat dem gegenwärtigen Herausgeber gezeigt, dass Konfliktrhythmen und agogische Akzente leichter zu fühlen und zu interpretieren sind bei regelmässigen Takten - die Chorsänger singen gegen die regelmässigen Taktstriche mit einem Gefühl für den Rhythmus.

DYNAMIK, TEMPO UND AUSDRUCKSZEICHEN: Aufführungsvorschriften sind nicht zugefügt, sodass Chordirigenten und Sänger reine Partituren haben, die sie interpretieren können, wie sie wollen. Gelegentlich, wo der Akzent in einem Konfliktrhythmus nicht unmittelbar deutlich ist, hat der Herausgeber eine kurze Linie (—) über oder unter die betreffende Note gesetzt.

TEXT UND WORTUNTERLEGUNG: Wo in den gedruckten Quellen der Text vollständig ist, ist er in den vorliegenden Ausgaben normal gedruckt, wo in diesen Quellen das Zeichen *ij* steht, um die Wiederholung einer Phrase anzuzeigen, sind die Worte in Kursivschrift gedruckt. Ein Vergleich der zwei Ausgaben der 4 stimmigen und der 3 stimmigen Messen hat den Herausgeber kaum im Zweifel über die Textunterlegung gelassen, weder im vollen Text noch in den Wiederholungen. Obwohl die gedruckten Quellen kleine

Anfangsbuchstaben anwenden für gewisse Worte, die sich auf die Gottheit beziehen (*Deus pater, agnus Dei, spiritus sancto* etc. etc.), bei denen man grosse Anfangsbuchstaben erwarten würde, drucken die 19 verschiedenen Stimmbücher der fünf Messeausgaben die Worte *Catholicam et Apostolicam Ecclesiam* im Glaubensbekenntnis konsequent mit grossen Anfangsbuchstaben, als ob dies eine besondere Bestätigung des Glaubens an die vergewaltigte Kirche wäre, eine Andeutung dafür, dass Byrd dementsprechende Vorschriften gegeben oder beim Korrekturlesen besonders darauf geachtet hat.

VORZEICHEN: Ein Studium der gedruckten Quellen, vor allem der ersten Ausgaben der 4 stimmigen und 3 stimmigen Messen hat den Herausgeber davon überzeugt, dass Byrd genau das meinte, was er druckte, und dass sehr wenig zugefügt werden muss soweit es die Vorzeichen betrifft. Die Vorzeichen, die in der vorliegenden Ausgabe vor die Noten gesetzt sind, stehen in den gedruckten Quellen. Der Herausgeber hat zwei Arten Vorzeichen zugefügt: (a) über den Noten, wo auch nur der geringste Zweifel besteht und wo die Erhöhung der Note unter dem Leitton entweder vergessen oder vorausgesetzt worden ist, und (b) in Klammern vor der Note, wo die Anwendung klar ist, z.B. bei der Rückkehr zur Originalnote der Tonart nach der Kadenz mit der Pikardischen Terz, oder als Warnungszeichen für den Sänger bei der Aufführung.

LIGATUREN: Obwohl der Gebrauch von Ligaturen und ihre Wirkung um diese Zeit etwas altertümlich, wenn nicht sogar veraltet war, sind die Stellen, wo sie vorkommen, durch eckige Klammern über den betreffenden Noten angezeigt.

INTONATIONEN: Zur Hilfe bei Aufführungen hat der Herausgeber die traditionellen Intonationen des cantus planus für *Gloria in excelsis* und *Credo*

vorgeschlagen, die sich für die äolische Tonart (4 stimmige und 5 stimmige Messen) und die ionische (3 stimmige Messe) eignen. Andere sind zu finden in: *Liber Usualis,* herausgegeben von den Benediktinern von Solesmes, Paris, etc. 1956, pp 16ff und 64ff.

TRANSPOSITION UND STIMMUMFANG: Der Umfang der Stimmen in jeder der Messen ist ungewöhnlich gross und umfasst offenbar Morleys hohe und tiefe Stimmung gleichzeitig. (*Plaine and Easie Introduction to Practicall Musick,* 1597, p. 166; Neudruck herausgegeben von R. A. Harman, 1952, p. 274f). Die 4 stimmige Messe ist einen ganzen Ton tiefer transponiert, wogegen die 3 stimmige und die 5 stimmige Messen in den originalen Tonarten gedruckt sind, also nicht transponiert. Der verstorbene H. D. Andrews bringt eine interessante und überzeugende Theorie über *chiavette* Transposition in *Transposition of Byrd's Vocal Polyphony.* (M & L 43, 1963, pp 25–37). Obwohl aus historischen und ästhetischen Gründen eine getreue heutige Transposition angewendet werden sollte, werden Chordirigenten (vor allem in Chören mit weiblichen Altstimmen) doch diese Werke in der Transposition aufführen, die sich für die grösste Stimmenanzahl eignet.

KAMMERORGEL CONTINUO UND BEGLEITUNG IN PROBEN: Der Herausgeber hat jede der Messen mit einer vereinfachten *reductio partiturae* versehen zur Hilfe für Chöre, die in Proben eine Unterstützung von einem Tasteninstrument brauchen. Ausserdem haben wir den historischen Beweis, dass Byrd in der Afführung dieser Messen eine Form von Continuo auf einem Tasteninstrument gebrauchte oder gebraucht wissen wollte. Dieser Beweis basiert auf der Aufführungspraxis der Kirchenmusik dieser Zeit und auf der Berücksichtigung des Zweckes, für den Byrd Musik für die geächteten katholischen Riten komponierte, wenn man seine veröffentlichten lateinischen Werke, ihre Tonhöhe und ihren Stimmumfang betrachtet. Die Orgelbücher in Christ Church, Durham, Peterhouse u.a. und die Tatsache, dass die Chapel Royal, Durham, York und andere Kathedralen und Stiftskirchen Ensembles von Zinken und Posaunen unterhielten zur Verdoppelung der Stimmen, sind Beweis genug, dass es nicht üblich war, Kirchenmusik ohne Begleitung aufzuführen. Die reformierten englischen Kirchen hatten keineswegs die Aufführung von lateinischen Werken verboten, dort, wo lateinisch verstanden wurde, aber im liturgischen Gottesdienst war es notwendig, sich an das *Booke of Common Praier* zu halten, und die lateinischen Werke, die nicht umstritten waren, hatten ihren Platz ausserhalb der Liturgie. In diese Kategorie kann man die *Cantiones Sacrae*, 1575, einreihen, die der Königin Elizabeth gewidmet waren, zu denen Tallis und Byrd je 17 Motetten beitrugen, und die 2 Bände *Sacrarum Cantionum*, 1589 und 1591, von denen einer 16, der andere 21 Motetten enthalten. Eine Analyse dieser 54 Motetten von Byrd zeigt—wohl nur mit Ausnahme von *Salve, Regina, Mater* (1591, No. 6)—, dass die Texte nicht umstritten waren und dass Tonhöhe und Stimmumfang so tief liegen, dass Byrd sie in Orgel- (oder Kirchen-) Stimmung geschrieben haben muss, mit der Möglichkeit, wenn nicht sogar der Absicht, sie in der reformierten Kirche aufzuführen; sie verlangen heute die Transposition einen ganzen Ton oder eine kleine Terz nach oben. Andererseits enthalten die zwei Bände *Gradualia*, 1605 und 1607, und ihre zweiten Auflagen von 1610, die Proprium Messe, (Introit, Gradual, Alleluia oder Tract, Offertory und Communion), wie auch gewisse Responsorien in den Vespern für die Feiertage eines ganzen Jahres, einschliesslich der Feiertage der Heiligen Jungfrau und anderer, die nicht im reformierten Gebetbuch stehen. Im Vorwort zum ersten Band *Gradualia* schreibt Byrd dass diese bestimmt sind: "for you who delight at times to sing to God in hymns and spiritual songs . . ." und man kann darüber streiten, ob nicht seine Absicht mehr als ein Wunschtraum war. Viel wahrscheinlicher ist allerdings, dass diese 107 Introits etc. in der Tat aufgeführt wurden, wenigstens teilweise, in geheimen Feiern der alten Riten in Herrensitzen und anderen Privathäusern, und dasselbe kann man auch bezüglich seiner Kompositionen der 4 stimmigen, 3 stimmigen und 5 stimmigen Messen annehmen. Dass die 4 stimmige und 3 stimmige Messen in einer 2. Auflage erschienen, ebenso wie *Gradualia* 10 Jahre später, könnte als zusätzlicher Beweis für die Nachfrage und ihren Gebrauch bei solchen Feiern ausgelegt und kann nicht nur als Wunschtraum abgetan werden. Eine Analyse der Stimmung und des Stimmumfangs der Messen und *Gradualia* reiht sie in die gleiche Kategorie ein, denn sie liegen im Stimmumfang des Kirchenchores (mit männlichen Altstimmen) ohne die übliche Transposition um einen Ganzton oder eine kleine Terz höher für heutige Aufführungen, und waren daher nicht in Orgelstimmung geschrieben (d.h. in der Stimmung der Orgeln in den reformierten Kirchen). Die Folgerung davon ist, dass die Messen und *Gradualia* in weltlicher Stimmung geschrieben wurden und dass sie, wenn sie überhaupt aufgeführt wurden, (was der Herausgeber für sehr wahrscheinlich hält) auf einer Kammerorgel begleitet wurden, gemäss der üblichen Aufführungspraxis der Kirchenmusik, oder wenn keine Orgel vorhanden war, von einem Gamben-Ensemble. (In dieser Analyse über Stimmung und Umfang ist die Möglichkeit in Betracht gezogen worden, dass Byrd in gewissen Einzelheiten in den *Gradualia* einen Unterschied machte zwischen hoher Lage—"*for more life*" und tiefer Lage—"*for more gravity and staidness*", wie sein Schüler Morley in der zeitgenössischen Veröffentlichung erklärt, und dass er in einigen Stücken die kirchentonartlichen Beschränkungen der jeweiligen Stimmen beachtete—zu dieser Zeit ein veralteter Brauch). Heutige Aufführungen der Messen und *Gradualia* verlangen dagegen häufig Transposition in eine tiefere Tonart, wie z.B. in der vorliegenden Ausgabe der 4 stimmigen Messe.

Chordirigenten werden natürlich die 3 Messen mit oder ohne Kammerorgel Continuo aufführen, wie sie es für richtig halten, aber wir hoffen dargelegt zu haben, dass die historische Tatsache des Orgelcontinuos mehr ist als eine Spekulation. Es ist nicht allgemein bekannt, dass die englische Tradition, Werke des 16. Jahrhunderts unbegleitet zu singen, nicht viel älter ist als die englische Renaissance am Ende des vorigen Jahrhunderts,— als Herausgeber anfingen, Bemerkungen zu machen wie: *Accomt. for practice only* (Rockstro & Squire, 4 stimmige Messe, 1890) and: *. . . should always be sung without accompaniment* (Squire, 3 stimmige Messe 1901). Die authentische Tradition des Singens mit Begleitung hat sich durch das 17. bis zum 19. Jahrhundert erhalten: John Immyns' MS Partitur der 3 stimmigen Messe, die er für seine Madrigal Society ca. 1750 anfertigte, hat einen bezifferten Bass (Fitzwilliam Museum MS *30.G.5.*) und die erste Ausgabe seit dem 16. Jahrhundert einer Byrd Messe (Rimbault, 5 stimmig, 1841) hat eine begleitende Orgelstimme von Macfarren. Die Orgelpartitur in Christ Church (*Ch.Ch. 1001*), anfangs des 17. Jahrhunderts geschrieben, enthält keine späteren Werke als die von Gibbons und ist nicht nur eine Abschrift von Stimmen, sondern fügt Verzierungen und durchgehende Noten nach Belieben ein. Der Continuospieler, der in einer heutigen Aufführung eine Orgel benutzt, sollte nach seinem Ermessen die Kammerorgelstimme des Herausgebers verzieren, z.B. indem er verzierte statt einfacher Auflösungen von dissonanten Akkorden spielt, und umgekehrt. Auf jeden Fall sollte der Continuo dünn sein und sich unauffällig mit den Stimmen mischen, das Pedal soll nicht benutzt werden.

Wer sich ernsthaft mit Byrds Stil befassen will, mag H. K. Andrews' hinterlassenes monumentales Werk lesen: *The Technique of Byrd's Vocal Polyphony*, pp. 306, 4°, OUP 1966, (568 musikalische Beispiele). Byrds Anwendung eines "Hauptmotives" in seinen Messen wird auf Seite 267 ff behandelt.

(Übers. Hilde Volhard)

FACSIMILE 1. **Mass for Four Voices**, 1st edition of 1592-3, ALTUS, ff.3ᵛ-4ʳ, Sanctus and Agnus Dei, (Christ Church Library, Oxford, Ch.Ch.489).

FACSIMILE 2. Mass for Four Voices, 2nd edition of c.1599, ALTUS, ff.3v-4r, Sanctus and Agnus Dei, (British Museum, K.8.d.11). Compare with equivalent pages of 1st edition, facsimile 1. Reproduced by courtesy of the Trustees of the British Museum.

These editions of Byrd's Masses

are dedicated to the memory of

Herbert Kennedy Andrews

M.A., D.Mus., F.R.C.O.

August 10th 1904 — October 10th 1965

Requiescat in pace

Mass for Four Voices

Transcribed from the 1st. edition of
1592-3 and edited by Frederick Hudson

William Byrd
1543-1623

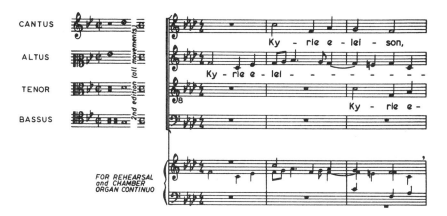

FOR REHEARSAL
and CHAMBER
ORGAN CONTINUO

No. 997   E. E. 6456   Ernst Eulenburg Ltd

4

Gloria in Excelsis

98

102

¹⁾ *It is suggested that a small group of tenors be added to the altos for this phrase and the next.*

106

__ so - lus al - tis - - - si - mus, tu

- mus, tu so -

tu so - lus al - tis - si - mus, al - tis - si - mus, tu

tu so - lus al - tis - - -

110

so - lus al - tis - si - mus, Ie - su Chri - - ste,

- lus al - tis - si - mus, Ie - su Chri - - ste,

so - lus al - tis - - si - mus, Ie - su Chri - ste,

- si - mus, al - tis - si - mus, Ie - su Chri - ste,

122

126

Credo

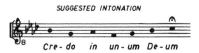

SUGGESTED INTONATION

Cre - do in un - um De - um

24

E. E. 6456

E. E. 6456

32

121

Et in Spi - ri-tum san - ctum, Do - mi-num, et

Et in Spi - ri-tum san - ctum, Do - mi-num, et

Et in Spi - ri-tum san - ctum, Do - mi-num,

Et in Spi - ri-tum san - ctum, Do - mi-num,

125

vi - vi-fi-can - tem, et vi - vi - fi - can-tem,

vi - vi-fi-can-tem, vi - vi-fi-can - tem, qui ex pa - tre fi -

et vi - vi-fi-can - tem qui ex pa - tre fi - li - o -

et vi - vi-fi-can - tem, qui

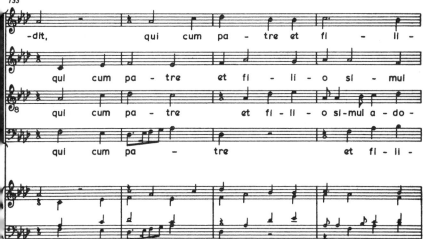

38

E. E. 6456

40

E. E. 6456

42

Sanctus

CANTUS

ALTUS

TENOR

BASSUS

46

Benedictus

Agnus Dei